Ice Pop Recipe Book: 99 Traditional Ice Pop Recipes For The Entire Family

JB Publishing

Published by JB Publishing, 2022.

While every precaution has been taken in the preparation of this book, the publisher assumes no responsibility for errors or omissions, or for damages resulting from the use of the information contained herein.

ICE POP RECIPE BOOK: 99 TRADITIONAL ICE POP RECIPES FOR THE ENTIRE FAMILY

First edition. March 1, 2022.

ISBN: 979-8201504311

Written by JB Publishing.

Table of Contents

To all the other busy moms and dads out there.

ICE POP
RECIPE BOOK
99 Traditional Ice Pop Recipes For The Entire Family

1 ICE POPS WITH YOGURT

Recipe No. 1

You need:

- 8 sticks for popsicles
- 8 paper cups
- Yogurt (2 cups)
- Sugar (quarter of a cup)
- Fresh fruit (fresh blueberries, strawberries, bananas, raspberries)

Preparation:

The preparation should last about 15 minutes. Put fruit, yogurt, and sugar in a blender. Blend it until completely mingled and smooth. Then pour this mixture into the cups, ¾ of the cup, and cover the cups with aluminum foil. Poke the sticks through the foils on the cups and put them in the freezer for 5 hours or more. When you want to serve the popsicles, just peel off the cups and remove the foils.

Recipe No. 2

You need:

  - 6 ice pop molds
  - Fresh strawberries (8 hulled and quartered)
  - Honey (2 tablespoons)
  - Apple juice (¼ cup)
  - Yogurt (¼ cup)

Preparation:

This preparation should last about 10 minutes. Put all the ingredients in the blender and blend until smooth. Then pour the mixture into the molds and freeze for about 12 hours.

Recipe No. 3

You need:

- 6 ice pop molds
- Vanilla yogurt (1 ½ cups)
- Sliced mango (1 cup)
- Banana (1 small)
- Orange (1 juiced)
- Pineapple chunks, undrained (1 can / 8 ounces)

Preparation:

This preparation should last about 10 minutes. Blend all the ingredients in a blender until smooth. Pour the mixture into the ice pop molds and freeze until firm – for about 4 to 6 hours.

Recipe No. 4

You need:

- 6 ice pop molds
- Frozen vanilla yogurt (2 cups)
- Fresh blackberries (8 ounces)
- Sugar (2 tablespoons)

Preparation:

This preparation should last about 30 minutes. Blend the fruit (blackberries) until smooth. You should filtrate the blended fruit through a fine sieve to remove the seeds. Then add sugar and yogurt and make the mixture smooth. Almost ready now, because all you have to do here is to pour this mixture into molds and freeze them for 3+ hours.

Recipe No. 5

You need:

- 6 ice pop molds
- Frozen cherries (1 cup)
- Frozen blueberries (1 cup)
- Greek yogurt (½ cup)
- Honey (3 tablespoons)
- Frozen chopped spinach (½ cup, thawed, drained)

Preparation:

This preparation should last about 10 minutes since it is very simple. Put the ingredients in the blender and mix until smooth. Pour the mixture into the ice pop molds and freeze for about 2 hours.

Recipe No. 6

You need:

- 10 ice pop molds
- Coconut extract (½ teaspoon)
- Coconut flakes (1 cup, sweetened)
- Nonfat vanilla yogurt (3 cups, not Greek yogurt)

Preparation:

This preparation should last about 10 minutes. Take a bowl and place yogurt, coconut extract and coconut flakes into it. Mix it and pour the mixture into the molds. Place the sticks into the pops and leave it in the freezer for about 6+ hours.

Recipe No. 7

You need:

- 6 ice pop molds
- Fresh strawberries (8 pieces, hulled, quartered)
- Yogurt (¼ cup)
- Apple juice (¼ cup)
- Honey (2 tablespoons)

Preparation:

This preparation should last about 10 minutes. Blend all the ingredients until smooth. Then pour the mixture into the molds. These popsicles should be in the freezer for at least 12 hours.

Recipe No. 8

You need:

- 8 ice pop molds
- 8 wooden sticks
- Blueberry juice cocktail (1 cup)
- Fresh blueberries (1 cup, cleaned and rinsed)
- Fat-free vanilla yogurt (1 container / 6 ounces)

Preparation:

This preparation should last for about 5 minutes. Blend all the ingredients until smooth. Pour this mixture into the mold, place the sticks and hold in the freezer for 2+ hours.

Recipe No. 9

You need:

 - 12 ice pop molds or plastic cups
 - Fresh blueberries (12 ounces)
 - Greek yogurt (1 container / 32 ounces)
 - Honey (1 tablespoon)

Preparation:

This preparation should last for about 10 minutes. Mix the ingredients in the blender until smooth. Pour the mixture into the molds/plastic cups and add some wooden sticks. Freeze for 4+ hours.

You need:

- 2 molds
- Frozen strawberries (8 pieces)
- Frozen blueberries (½ cup)
- Vanilla sugar-free yogurt (¾ cup)

Preparation:

This preparation should last about 5 minutes, just as much you need to blend the ingredients until smooth. Place the thick mixture into the molds and eat immediately. It doesn't have to be frozen! But you could freeze it if you want to.

<h1 style="text-align:center">Recipe No. 11</h1>

You need:

- 6 ice pop molds
- Sugar (2 tablespoons)
- Grapefruit juice (½ cup)
- Orange juice (1 cup)
- Strawberries (½ cup, chopped)
- Water (¼ cup)
- Vanilla yogurt (1 container / 8 ounces)
- Lemon juice (2 tablespoons)

Preparation:

This preparation should last about 15 minutes. You should take a saucepan and pour all the juices, water and sugar. This mixture should boil a bit until the sugar is dissolved. Then put this mixture in the freezer for about 10 minutes. On the other side mix strawberries and yogurt. Then take the mixture from the freezer and place a bit of it into the molds (about 1½ tablespoon of it). Then place the molds in the freezer for about 1 hour +/- and afterward put a layer of strawberry-yogurt mixture on it (1 tablespoon). On the top, pour the remaining amount of the juice mixture. Then return the molds to the freezer and leave them there for another hour or two.

Recipe No. 12

You need:

- 6 ice pop molds

- Plain yogurt ($^{2/3}$ cup)
- Cottage cheese (½ cup)
- Sugar (6 tablespoons)
- Fresh raspberries (3 cups)

Preparation:

This preparation should last about 10 minutes. You should blend the raspberries and pour them through a sieve to remove the seeds. Then continue the blending process together with all the other ingredients. When the mixture becomes smooth, place it into the molds. Place the sticks on the right places and freeze the molds for about 4+ hours.

Recipe No. 13

You need:

- 12 ice pop molds
- Greek yogurt (1 cup)
- Vanilla extract (½ teaspoon)
- Stevia powder (5 packets / 1 gram)
- Strawberries (1 cup)
- Raspberries (1 cup)
- Blueberries (1 cup)

Preparation:

This preparation should last about 10 minutes. Blend all the ingredients until the mixture becomes smooth. Pour the mixture into the molds, place the sticks and freeze them for about 4+ hours.

Recipe No. 14

You need:

- 10 ice pop molds
- Sugar (2 tablespoons)
- Vanilla extract (½ teaspoon)
- Orange juice (1½ cups)
- Low-fat vanilla yogurt

Preparation:

This preparation should last about 10 minutes. You should whisk sugar, vanilla, yogurt, and juice and then the mixture is ready to be placed in the molds. Fill the molds, place the sticks, and freeze for about 6+ hours.

Recipe No. 15

You need:

- 6 ice pop molds
- Pure maple syrup (1 tablespoon)
- Frozen strawberries (2 cups)
- Pomegranate juice or cranberry juice cocktail (½ cup)
- Strawberry yogurt (1 cup)
- 1 banana

Preparation:

This preparation should last about 10 minutes. Blend all the ingredients until smooth and then pour the mixture into the molds. Freeze them for more than 6 hours.

You need:

- 6 ice pop molds
- Honey (¼ cup)
- Greek yogurt (1 ¼ cup)
- Peaches (1 ½ cups, diced)
- Water (3 tablespoons)

Preparation:

This preparation should last about 20 minutes. Place honey, peaches, and water in the bowl, cover it, poke some holes in the cover, and place the bowl in the microwave. Heat it for 2 minutes, take it out, stir it a bit, and return in the microwave for 2 minutes more. Take the bowl out and let it cool a bit. Take the blender and pour this mixture into it together with yogurt. Blend the mixture until it becomes smooth. Then this mixture is ready to be placed in the molds and frozen for 6 + hours.

II POPSICLES WITH SPECIAL MILK

Recipe No. 17

You need:

- 10 plastic cups or molds
- Fat-free milk (½ cup)
- Vanilla pudding (1 package)
- Fresh raspberries (1 cup)
- Softened raspberry sherbet (2 cups)
- Frozen whipped thawed topping (2 cups)

Preparation:

This preparation should last about 15 minutes. Take a bowl and pour 1 cup of milk in it to be used for making pudding. Beat it with mixer for about 2 minutes. Add the raspberry puree and whipped topping. Mix it until mingled completely. Then add the softened sherbet which can be mixed in completely or left swirled – it is optional. Pour this mixture into the plastic cups or molds and poke some wooden sticks into each. Place the cups/molds into the freezer for 3 or more hours.

Recipe No. 18

You need:

- 6 ice pop molds
- Coconut milk (1 can /14 ounces)
- Sugar (3 tablespoons)
- Banana (1 chopped)
- Pineapple (1 can /8 ounces, crushed)
- Kiwi (1 cup, chopped)

Preparation:

This preparation should last about 10 minutes. Take a bowl and mix milk with sugar. Then pour this mixture into the blender together with banana and pineapple and blend until smooth. Pour the mixture into molds and press kiwi fruit into it. When you've done this, put the pops into the freezer and let them stay there for 8+ hours.

Recipe No. 19

You need:

- 6 ice pop molds
- Coconut milk (1 can / 10 ounces)
- Pineapple chunks (1 can / 4 ounces, juiced)
- 1 Banana
- Vanilla extract (½ teaspoon)

Preparation:

This preparation should last about 10 minutes. Blend all the ingredients until smooth. Then pour the mixture into the molds and freeze for about 4 hours.

Recipe No. 20

You need:

- 12 paper cups
- Vanilla soy milk (2½ cups)
- Blueberries (1 pint)
- Strawberries (1 pint, hulled)
- Brown sugar (½ cup)

Preparation:

This preparation should last about 15 minutes. Blend the fruits – blueberries, and strawberries – and strain the mixture through a sieve lined with cheesecloth to remove the seeds. Mix it with brown sugar and soy milk in the blender. When blended smooth, pour the mixture into paper cups and place them in the freezer until firm. Then poke the wooden sticks into them and freeze for 3 hours more.

Recipe No. 21

You need:

- 10 ice pop molds
- Pineapple juice (1 ½ cups)
- Frozen mango chunks (1 ½ cups)
- Frozen pineapple chunks (1 cup)
- Granulated sugar (2 tablespoons)
- Dairy whipped topping (2 cups)
- Coconut extract (¾ teaspoon)

Preparation:

This preparation should last about 15 minutes. Take the blender and put mango, pineapple juice, pineapple chunks, sugar, topping, and coconut extract in it. Blend it until smooth. When finished, pour the mixture into the molds and insert sticks. Freeze for 8+ hours.

Recipe No. 22

You need:

- 8 ice pop molds
- Coconut milk (½ cup)
- Agave nectar (¼ cup)
- Lime juice (¼ cup)
- Vanilla extract (2 teaspoons)
- Avocado (1, peeled and pitted)
- Salt (¼ teaspoon)

Preparation:

This preparation should last about 10 minutes. Blend the ingredients until smooth. Pour the mixture into the molds and freeze for 2+ hours.

Recipe No. 23

You need:

- 10 ice pop molds
- Sweetened condensed milk (1 cup)
- Normal milk (1 cup)
- White rice (1 cup)
- Water (2 cups)
- Sugar (1 cup)

Preparation:

This preparation should last about 15 minutes. Put rice, sugar, and water in a saucepan, cover it, and simmer on a medium-low temperature until the rice gets tender and the water evaporates (about 15-20 minutes). Mix this mixture with condensed milk and normal milk and put this new mixture into molds. The freezing process should last more than 2 hours.

Recipe No. 24

You need:

- 10 ice pop molds
- Light coconut milk (1 can / 13.5 ounces)
- Fat-free evaporated milk (1 can / 12 fluid ounces)
- Coconut extract (2 teaspoons)
- Confectioners' sugar (½ cup)
- A bit of cinnamon to taste

Preparation:

This preparation should last about 5 minutes. All the ingredients should be whisked together. Then this mixture should be poured into the molds and the molds placed in the freezer. This tasty pops should stay in the freezer for about 4 hours or more.

Recipe No. 25

You need:

- 10 ice pop molds
- Vanilla extract (¼ teaspoon)
- Coconut (½ cup, shredded)
- Pineapple (½ cup, minced)
- Coconut milk (1 can / 14 ounces)
- Sweetened condensed milk (½ can / 14 ounces)
- Salt (¼ teaspoon)
- Half-and-half cream (¾ cup)

Preparation:

This preparation should last for about 10 minutes. Take a blender and pour milk, put cream, condensed milk, vanilla extract, and salt and blend until smooth. Then stir pineapple and shredded coconut into this mixture. So, it is almost finished now just pour this mixture into the molds and freeze them for about 4+ hours.

Recipe No. 26

You need:

- 8 ice pop molds
- Vanilla extract (2 teaspoons)
- Cocoa powder (2 teaspoons, unsweetened)
- Pitted dates (6 pieces)
- Bananas (3, ripe)
- Coconut milk (¾ can / 13.5 ounces)
- Almond milk (¼ cup)
- A bit of salt

Preparation:

This preparation should last about 15 minutes. Take a bowl and put dates in it together with a bit of hot water to make them soft. After 6 to 10 minutes drain the dates and place them in the blender together with bananas, almond milk, coconut milk, cocoa powder, vanilla, and salt. Blend them until smooth. Pour this mixture into molds and freeze for about 6+ hours).

Recipe No. 27

You need:

- 6 ice pop molds
- Coconut milk (1 cup, canned)
- Raw honey (3 tablespoons)
- Orange juice (1 cup, freshly squeezed)
- Vanilla extract (½ teaspoon)

Preparation:

This preparation should last about 15 minutes. Whisk all the ingredients and pour this mixture into the molds. Place the sticks and freeze for about 8+ hours.

Recipe No. 28

You need:

- 6 ice pop molds
- Vanilla-flavored almond milk (1 cup)
- Honey (1 tablespoon)
- Bananas (2 large ones)

Preparation:

This preparation should last about 10 minutes. You should blend almond milk, honey, and bananas until smooth. Then pour this mixture into the molds and freeze for about 8+ hours.

Recipe No. 29

You need:

- 10 ice pop molds
- A bit of salt
- Low-fat milk (2 cups)
- Vanilla extract (2 teaspoons)
- Bananas (2 cups / 2 pieces diced)
- Brown sugar (½ cup)
- Cornstarch (2 tablespoons)

Preparation:

This preparation should last about 20 minutes. Take a saucepan and place the sugar, salt, and cornstarch in it together with milk. Stir this mixture until it becomes smooth. Then make it boil over a medium heat for about 1 minute. Then add vanilla in it. Put half of this mixture in the blender and blend it with bananas. The rest of the mixture should be added after the blending process. Place the final mixture into the molds, add sticks, and freeze for about 6 hours.

III POPSICLES WITH CHOCOLATE

Recipe No. 30

You need:

- 8 ice pop molds
- Sugar (½ cup)
- Butter (1 tablespoon)
- Milk (2 ½ cups)
- Cocoa powder (2 tablespoons)
- Cornstarch (2 tablespoons)
- Vanilla extract (1 teaspoon)
- Chocolate chips (¼ cup miniature, semisweet)

Preparation:

This preparation should last about 10 minutes. You should mix sugar, cocoa powder, cornstarch, and milk in a saucepan over medium heat. Put it in a simmer and stir for about 2 minutes. When removed from the heat it should be stirred in vanilla and butter. Afterward, transfer it to a heatproof bowl and put it in the refrigerator for about 20 minutes. The chocolate chips should be stirred into the cooled chocolate mixture. Then pour it into the molds and keep in the freezer for about 4 hours.

Recipe No. 31

You need:

- 8 ice pop molds or small plastic cups
- Sugar (½ cup)
- Instant chocolate pudding mix (1 package / 3.9 ounces)
- Milk (3 cups)

Preparation:

This preparation should last about 15 minutes. Take a bowl and mix all the ingredients. When the mixture becomes smooth, pour it into molds or plastic cups. Put the cups/molds into the freezer for 3 hours sharp and they will be ready to be served.

Recipe No. 32

You need:

- 4 ice pop molds
- Chocolate-hazelnut spread – Nutella (¼ cup)
- Milk (½ cup)
- Whipped cream (1 cup)

Preparation:

This preparation should last about 10 minutes. Take a blender and mix chocolate-hazelnut spread, whipped cream, and milk until smooth (for about 2 minutes). Then pour this mixture into the molds and freeze it for about 3 hours.

Recipe No. 33

You need:

- Chopped walnuts (¼ cup)
- Chocolate chips (1 bag / 12 ounces)
- Bananas (4 pieces, cut in half, crosswise)
- Candy sprinkles (¼ cup)

Preparation:

This preparation should last about 20 minutes. Put the chocolate chips into a microwave for about 2 minutes until they barely melt and then stir them smooth. Mix the walnuts and the sprinkles into separate bowls. Then you should take the bananas and dip each one in melted chocolate and roll them in the other two bowls with sprinkles and walnuts. Put these bananas on waxed paper and put in the freezer for about 5-10 minutes until the chocolate becomes firm. Eat immediately. This is the recipe for 8 people.

Recipe No. 34

You need:

- 10 ice pop molds
- Sugar (4 tablespoons)
- Raspberries (2 cups)
- Yogurt (2 cups)
- Chocolate chips (½ cups)

Preparation:

This preparation should last about 15 minutes. Blend the yogurt, raspberries, and sugar until the mixture becomes smooth. Pour the mixture into the molds and then add chocolate chips equally to every mold. Stir it a bit and leave the molds to freeze for about 6 hours.

Recipe No. 35

You need:

- 6 ice pop molds
- Milk (3 cups)
- Chocolate pudding mix (1 pack)
- Sugar (½ cup)

Preparation:

This preparation should last about 15 minutes. Mix the pudding with milk and sugar until smooth. Pour this mixture into the molds and freeze them for 6+ hours.

Recipe No. 36

You need:

- 8 ice pop molds
- Vanilla extract (1 tablespoon)
- Avocado (1½ piece)
- Sugar (½ cup)
- Banana (2 pieces)
- Greek yogurt (1 cup)
- Cocoa powder (¼ cup)

Preparation:

This preparation should last about 15 minutes. Take the blender and blend all the ingredients until smooth. Pour the mixture into the molds and wait for 4+ hours to become completely frozen.

Recipe No. 37

You need:

- 6 ice pop molds
- Milk (½ cup)
- Honey (1 tablespoon)
- Greek yogurt (½ cup)
- Banana (4, frozen)
- Cocoa powder (1 ½ tablespoons)
- Vanilla (1 teaspoon)

Preparation:

This preparation should last about 25 minutes. You should blend 2 bananas, ¼ Greek yogurt, honey, ¼ cup of milk, and vanilla. Mix it until smooth and pour the mixture into the molds. Freeze the molds for about 1 hour. After about 45 minutes, blend the rest of the ingredients for the second layer. Take the molds from the freezer and pour the second layer. Return them to the freezer to continue the freezing process.

Recipe No. 38

You need:

- 8 ice pop molds
- Milk (2 cups)
- Chocolate chips (½ cups)
- Marshmallows (½ cup)
- Almonds (¼ cup, sliced)
- Instant chocolate pudding (1 package)

Preparation:

This preparation should last about 15 minutes. Prepare the pudding as required by the instructions. Then put a few marshmallows into the molds together with chocolate chips. Place one tablespoon of pudding over them and continue with the next layer of marshmallows, chocolate chips, and almonds. Then again add the pudding layer until you fill the molds. Freeze the molds for more than 6 hours.

You need:

- 6 ice pop molds
- Milk (1 cup)
- Sugar (1 tablespoon)
- Water (¼ cup)
- Cocoa powder (1 tablespoon)
- Chocolate chips (¾ cup)

Preparation:

This preparation should last about 15 minutes. Simmer sugar, water, milk, and cocoa for about 5 minutes. Pour this mixture over the chocolate chips and stir it until chips dissolve. Let it sit for 5 minutes and then pour this mixture into the molds. Freeze the molds for 6 hours.

Recipe No. 40

You need:

- 6 ice pop molds
- Honey (3 tablespoons)
- Cacao powder ($1/3$ cup)
- Vanilla extract (1 teaspoon)
- Coconut milk (1 can)

Preparation:

This preparation should last about 5 minutes. Mix all the ingredients in the blender and make it smooth. Pour the mixture into the molds and leave them in the freezer for about 4 hours.

Recipe No. 41

You need:

- 6 ice pop molds
- Coconut oil (tablespoons)
- Strawberries (2 cups)
- Dark chocolate (2 packages)
- Lemon juice (1 tablespoons)
- Water ($2/3$ cup)
- Honey (5 tablespoons)

Preparation:

This preparation should last about 10 minutes. Take a blender and place strawberries, honey, and lemon juice in it. Blend them until the mixture becomes smooth. Pour this mixture into the molds and place them in the freezer for about 4 hours. Then put the chocolate into coconut oil and melt it over the heater or in a microwave. Take the popsicles out of the molds and dip them in chocolate. Let the chocolate freeze for 1 hour and then you can serve them.

Recipe No. 42

You need:

- 8 ice pop molds
- Some sweetener of choice
- Milk (1 cup)
- A bit of salt
- Bananas (1 ½ ripe ones)
- Peanut butter (¼ cup + 2 tablespoons)
- Chocolate (1 package) or chocolate chips

Preparation:

This preparation should last about 5 minutes. Take all the ingredients and blend them until the mixture becomes smooth. Then just pour the mixture into the molds. Leave the molds in the freezer for about 1 hour to freeze. I the meantime, prepare the chocolate coating by melting the chocolate or by using chocolate chips. Dip the popsicles into the coating and freeze them for 5 more hours.

IV POPSICLES WITH ALCOHOL

Recipe No. 43

You need:

- 6 ice pop molds
- Sugar (¾ cup)
- Water (½ cup)
- Fresh strawberries ($1^{1/3}$ cups)
- Fresh blueberries ($1^{1/3}$ cups)
- Vodka (4 tablespoons)
- Softened cream cheese (4 ounces)

Preparation:

This preparation should last about 15 minutes. Take a saucepan and whisk sugar and water in it over medium heat. After 2 or 3 minutes sugar will be dissolved and syrup clear. Then cool this syrup to normal room temperature. Take a blender and fill it with previously prepared 1½ tablespoons of vodka, 1½ tablespoons of syrup and strawberries until the mixture becomes smooth. Pour this mixture into ice pop molds and freeze for at least 1 hour. After this time, take another bowl and pour 1½ tablespoons of syrup, cream cheese, and 1 tablespoon of vodka and whisk it until smooth. Pour this mixture over the first layer in the molds and return the molds to the freezer for another hour. After this second hour is over, blend blueberries together with 1½ tablespoons of vodka and 1½ tablespoons of syrup until smooth. Pour this third layer over the second one and freeze the ice pops overnight (for 8 hours).

Recipe No. 44

You need:

- 6 ice pop molds
- Lemon zest (1 teaspoon)
- Lemon juice (1½ tablespoon)
- Sugar (6 tablespoons)
- Water (7 tablespoons)
- Raspberries (3¼ cups, thawed)
- Wine (½ cup)

Preparation:

This preparation should last about 15 minutes. You should mash raspberries with a fork and stir in sugar and water. Then cover the bowl with the cover which can be used in the microwave, poke some holes in it, and heat it in the microwave for about 1½ minute. Then take it out, stir it, and heat it again for 1 minute. Take it out of the microwave and let it cool a bit. This mixture should be strained through a fine sieve. After this, stir it with wine, lemon zest, lemon juice, and water. The mixture is now ready to be placed in the molds and frozen for about 6 hours.

Recipe No. 45

You need:

- 6 ice pop molds
- Peach puree (1 cup)
- Bourbon (2 tablespoons)

Preparation:

This preparation should last about 5 minutes. You should blend all the ingredients until smooth and place the mixture into the molds. Freeze the molds for 8-12 hours.

Recipe No. 46

You need:

- 8 ice pop molds
- Rose wine (2 tablespoons)
- 1 papaya

Preparation:

This preparation should take about 5 minutes. Clean the papaya and scoop out the flesh. Blend the papaya flesh with wine and pour this mixture into the molds. Freeze for about 8-12 hours.

Recipe No. 47

You need:

- 8 ice pop molds
- Brandy (2 tablespoons)
- 1 nectarine
- White grape juice (¾ cup)
- Some orange liqueur (3 tablespoons)
- Cherries (16 small)
- Sweet green table grapes (20 small)

Preparation:

This preparation should last about 2-3 hours. Mix all the ingredients and leave the mixture in a bowl for 2-3 hours to sit in the refrigerator. Then pour the mixture in the molds and leave them in the freezer overnight.

<h1 style="text-align:center">Recipe No. 48</h1>

You need:

- 8 ice pop molds
- White rum (4 tablespoons)
- Cubed watermelon (2 ½ tablespoons)
- Lemon juice (3 tablespoons)
- Simple syrup (3 tablespoons)
- Spearmint leaves (12 large ones)

Preparation:

This preparation should last about 5 minutes. You should blend all the ingredients until fully mixed. Pour the mixture into the molds and insert the sticks after one hour of freezing. Continue the freezing process for about 8 hours.

Recipe No. 49

You need:

- 8 ice pop molds
- Kiwi (4 kiwis)
- Fresh mint (1 ½ teaspoon)
- Fresh ginger (2 teaspoons)
- Mango (1 ripe)
- Limeade (1 cup)

Preparation:

This preparation should last about 5 minutes. You should blend all the ingredients and pour the mixture into the molds. Leave the molds in the freezer for 8-12 hours to fully freeze.

Recipe No. 50

You need:

- 8 ice pop molds
- Pineapple (1 medium size)
- Sugar (1 cup)
- Rum (3 tablespoons)
- Water (½ cup)
- Coconut milk (1 container)

Preparation:

This preparation should last about 5 minutes. Blend all the ingredients for 1 minute and then pour it through a fine sieve. Then fill the molds and freeze them for 6+ hours.

Recipe No. 51

You need:

- 10 ice pop molds
- Water (½ cup)
- Tequila ($^{1/3}$ cup)
- Lime juice (½ cup)
- Sugar (½ cup)
- Grapefruit juice (2 ½ cups)
- A bit of sea salt

Preparation:

This preparation should last about 15 minutes. You should dissolve sugar in water over a heat and leave it to cool. Take a bowl and mix the juices with tequila, sea salt, and add this sweet syrup. Pour this mixture into the molds and freeze a bit until it becomes firm. Then insert the sticks and continue with the freezing process for about 12 hours.

Recipe No. 52

You need:

- 10 ice pop molds
- Vodka (4 tablespoons)
- Pineapple (½, not the whole one)
- Raspberries (15 pieces)
- Some pomegranate liqueur (2 tablespoons)

Preparation:

This preparation should last about 10 minutes. First, you should blend the pineapple with vodka. Separately, blend raspberries with pomegranate liqueur. Take the molds and into each one place about 1 ½ tablespoon of the first mixture, then the same amount of the second mixture and so on. Freeze the molds for about 8 – 12 hours.

Recipe No. 53

You need:

- 8 ice pop molds
- Water (¼ cup)
- Tequila ($1/3$ cup)
- Sugar (¼ cup)
- Fresh mint ($1/3$ cup)
- Watermelon (4 cups)
- Juice of 2 limes

Preparation:

This preparation should last about 15 minutes. Mix sugar, mint, and water and make it boil until sugar dissolves. Let it cool for about half an hour and then strain it through a fine sieve. On the other side, blend watermelon with the lime juice and strain through a fine sieve to remove all the seeds. Mix this with the previously made syrup and tequila. Pour this mixture into the molds. Freeze a bit, add the sticks and continue the freezing process for 12 hours.

Recipe No. 54

You need:

- 6 ice pop molds
- Simple syrup (¾ cup)
- Cantaloupe (1, peeled and seeded)
- Campari (¼ cup)

Preparation:

This preparation should last about 20 minutes. You should cut the cantaloupe into large parts and puree it. Mix the puree with the simple syrup and add Campari. Stir this mixture well and pour it into the molds. Freeze the mold for about one hour and then insert the sticks. Continue the freezing process for about 12 hours.

Recipe No. 55

You need:

- 12 ice pop molds
- Water (1 cup)
- Sugar (1 cup)
- Campari (½ cup)
- Grapefruit juice (3 cups)

Preparation:

This preparation should last about 15 minutes. The first thing you should do here is making the simple syrup. So, mix the water and sugar and let it boil for about 5 minutes. Then cool the syrup and on the other side mix the citrus juice and Campari and then combine it with syrup. Now you only have to pour this mixture into the molds, add sticks after one hour of freezing and continue the process for about 10-12 hours.

You need:

- 8 ice pop molds
- Cherry beer (¾ cup)
- Chopped cherries (2 cups)
- Heavy cream (2 tablespoons and ¼ cup)
- Sugar (2 tablespoons)

Preparation:

This preparation should last about 15 minutes. Mix the cherries and sugar in the blender and blend until the mixture is smooth. Pour it slowly into the cherry beer and leave it for a while until bubbles vanish. On the other side, mix the heavy cream and sugar. Now, take the molds and do the following: take a few tablespoons of the mixture with cream and place them in the molds. Then follows the layer of the other mixture and so on until you use up the whole amount. Place the molds in the freezer, add sticks after a while and leave them to freeze for about 10-12 hours.

Recipe No. 57

You need:

- 6 ice pop molds
- Sugar (¾ cup)
- Raspberry (4 cups, fresh)
- Lemon zest (from 1 lemon)
- Champagne (½ cup)

Preparation:

This preparation should last about 10 minutes. You should blend raspberries with sugar. Then add lemon zest and champagne and stir it for 1 minute. Pour the mixture into the molds and freeze them for about 8+ hours or overnight.

V POPSICLES WITH COOKIES

Recipe No. 58

You need:

- 8 ice pop molds
- Sugar (2 tablespoons)
- Water (2 tablespoons)
- Vanilla sandwich cookies (8 pieces)
- Strawberries (8, hulled)
- Milk (2 cups)
- Cheesecake flavor pudding (1 package / 3.4 ounces)

Preparation:

This preparation should last about 10 minutes. Blend the cookies entirely. Separately blend water, strawberries, and sugar until smooth. Take a bowl and mix pudding and milk in it for about 2 minutes. Combine it with blended cookies. Pour 1/3 of the molds with this pudding-cookie mixture and the remaining 2/3 fill with strawberry mixture. Put sticks in the molds and keep them in the freezer for about 8 hours.

Recipe No. 59

You need:

- 8 ice pop molds
- Water (¼ cup)
- Milk (¼ cup)
- Vanilla extract (tablespoon)
- Sugar (¼ cup)
- Heavy cream (1 cup)
- Chocolate cookies (15 pieces)
- Sour cream (½ cup)

Preparation:

This preparation should last about 20 minutes. Take a bowl and crumble the cookies to very small pieces. In the other bowl, stir together water and sugar until sugar dissolves. Then add milk, sour cream, heavy cream, and vanilla. After this, stir in the crumbled cookies and pour the final mixture into the molds. Freeze the molds for 1 hour, add sticks, and continue the freezing process for 6 hours.

Recipe No. 60

You need:

- 8 ice pop molds
- Sugar (2 tablespoons)
- Milk (¾ cup)
- Cool whip topping (½ cup)
- Cookies (your favorite)

Preparation:

This preparation should last about 10 minutes. Take the blender and mix the topping, sugar, and milk. Crumble the cookies into this mixture and stir it a bit. Then pour this mixture into the molds and place them in the freezer for about half an hour. Then add the sticks and leave them in the freezer overnight.

Recipe No. 61

You need:

- 10 ice pop molds
- Milk (1 ½ cup)
- Vanilla extract (1 teaspoon)
- Heavy cream (1 cup)
- Sugar (2 tablespoons)
- Sandwich cookies (1 package)

Preparation:

This preparation should last about 10 minutes. Take a bowl and mix sugar, milk, cream, and vanilla extract. Whisk it until the sugar dissolves completely. Then take the molds and crumble the cookies into them. Pour the prepared mixture over the cookies and place the molds into the freezer for about 8 hours.

Recipe No. 62

You need:

- Whole milk (1 cup)

- Condensed milk ($2/3$ cup)
- Chocolate chip cookies (14 medium sized)
- Vanilla extract (½ teaspoon)

Preparation:

This preparation should last about 10 minutes. You should mix the two kinds of milk and put the mixture into the microwave for about 1 minute. Add vanilla and stir it well. Crush the cookies and put a small amount of them into the molds, then pour this mixture over the cookies. Don't fill the molds up to the end since the mixture will expand as it freezes. Let the molds stay in the freezer for about 6-8 hours.

Recipe No. 63

You need:

- 6 ice pop molds
- Sugar (1 tablespoon)
- Heavy whipping cream ($2/3$ cup)
- 8 cookies
- Vanilla (1 teaspoon)

Preparation:

This preparation should last about 10 minutes. Take a large bowl and mix cream, cookies, and sugar. Pour this mixture into the molds and add some little pieces of cookies on the top. Freeze for one hour, add sticks and then freeze for 5 hours more.

Recipe No. 64

You need:

- 8 ice pop molds
- Black-and-white cookies (1 package)
- Sugar (2 tablespoons)
- Heavy cream (½ cup)
- Milk (1½ cup)
- Unsweetened cocoa powder (2 tablespoons)

Preparation:

This preparation should last about 2h and 15 minutes. Divide the cookies – separate black ones from the white ones. Take a bowl and mix half the amount of heavy cream, milk, and sugar with the white cookies. When this mixture becomes smooth, pour it into the molds up to ½ of the molds. Add some small pieces of black cookies in it and freeze the molds for 2 hours. In the meantime mix the remaining amounts of the ingredients with cocoa powder and the black cookies. Blend until it becomes smooth and pour the mixture over the previously made and frozen layer in the molds. Now, freeze the molds for 4+ hours.

Recipe No. 65

You need:

- 6 ice pop molds
- Full-fat sweetened condensed milk (1 can)
- Fat-free milk (1 cup)
- 10 crushed cookies

Preparation:

This preparation should last about 5 minutes. Crush the cookies into the molds. Then blend the milk and pour the mixture over the cookies. Freeze the molds up to 10 hours.

Recipe No. 66

You need:

- 8 ice pop molds
- Milk (1¼ cup)
- Icing sugar (¼ cup)
- Vanilla extract (1 teaspoon)
- Pouring cream (½ cup)
- 16 cream-filled chocolate cookies

Preparation:

This preparation should last about 10 minutes. Take a bowl and whisk sugar, cream, milk, and vanilla until sugar becomes completely dissolved. Add crumbled cookies and stir it a bit. Pour the mixture into the molds and leave them in the freezer for 6 hours.

Recipe No. 67

You need:

- 6 ice pop molds
- 12 cookies
- Milk (½ cup)
- Plain yogurt (2 tablespoons)
- Light whipping cream (½ cup)
- Honey (2 tablespoons)

Preparation:

This preparation should last about 20 minutes. Place the whole cookies into the molds – one cookie per mold. Mix milk with whipping cream, yogurt, and honey. Pour this mixture over the cookies in the molds. Freeze the molds overnight.

Recipe No. 68

You need:

- 8 ice pop molds
- Whole milk ($1/3$ cup)
- Sour cream (¼ cup)
- Sugar (¾ cup)
- Butter (1 tablespoon, melted)
- Strawberries (7 large ones, chopped)
- Crackers (20 pieces or whole package)
- Cream cheese (1 cup)

Preparation:

This preparation should last about 10 minutes. Blend sour cream, cream cheese, and sugar until the sugar dissolves. Then add strawberries and stir them into the mixture. Take this mixture and pour it into the molds leaving about 2cm from the top empty. Place the molds in the freezer for about 15 minutes. In the meantime, blend the crackers and place them over the mixture in the molds. Continue the freezing process for about 6 hours.

VI POPSICLES MADE WITH AVOCADO

Recipe No. 69

You need:

- 8 ice pop molds
- Water (warm, 1 cup)
- Avocado (2, diced)
- Agave nectar (½ cup)
- Fresh lime juice (3 tablespoons)
- Salt (1 pinch)

Preparation:

This preparation should last about 5 minutes. Start with dissolving agave nectar in the warm water. Then pour this mixture into the blender and add the fruits and salt. Blend until smooth. It is finished now, just pour it into the molds and freeze for about 6 hours.

<h1 style="text-align:center">Recipe No. 70</h1>

You need:

- 10 ice pop molds
- Avocado (3 peeled and pitted)
- Lime (1, juiced)
- Water (1 cup)
- Sugar (½ cup)
- Salt (¼ teaspoon)

Preparation:

This preparation should last about 20 minutes. Mix water with sugar and make it boil until dissolved completely. After this solution cools, blend it with avocados, lime juice, and salt until the mixture becomes smooth. Then pour the mixture into the molds. Freeze for about 2 hours until they become firm and insert wooden sticks. Afterward, return them to the freezer for more than 12 hours.

You need:

- 8 ice pop molds
- Coconut milk (1 cup)
- 1 fresh avocado
- Lemon juice (2 tablespoons)
- Honey (2 tablespoons)
- Coconut (¼ cup sweetened, shredded)

Preparation:

This preparation should last about 10 minutes. Prepare avocado and place it in a blender together with milk, honey, and lemon juice. Blend until smooth. Then pour the mixture into the molds and freeze for about 1 hour until you add the sticks, then continue the freezing process for 5 hours.

You need:

- 10 ice pop molds
- Sweetened condensed milk (4 tablespoons)
- Avocado (3 ripe ones)
- Milk (1½ cup)
- Simple syrup
- Chocolate (1 dark one)

Preparation:

This preparation should last about 4 hours. Take a blender and mix avocado flesh, milk, condensed milk, and simple syrup. Pour this mixture into the molds and freeze for about 3 hours. In the meantime, melt the chocolate. Take out the popsicles from the molds and dip them into the chocolate or drizzle the chocolate over the popsicles. Return them to the freezer for about 45 minutes so that the chocolate freezes completely.

Recipe No. 73

You need:

- 10 ice pop molds
- Honey (3 tablespoons)
- Coconut milk (1 can)
- Coconut oil (½ cup)
- Avocado (2 large ones)
- Dark chocolate (1 package)
- Walnuts ($1/3$ cup)

Preparation:

This preparation should last about 4 hours. Blend avocado meat, coconut milk, and honey until the mixture become smooth. Pour this mixture into the molds and place the sticks. Freeze the molds for about 3 hours. Then melt the chocolate with coconut oil until it becomes smooth. Take the popsicles out of the molds and dip them in this chocolate mixture. Freeze the popsicles for 1 more hour.

Recipe No. 74

You need:

- 6 ice pop molds
- Lime juice (2 tablespoons)
- Grated lime rind (½ teaspoon)
- A bit of salt
- Water (¾ cup)
- Sugar (6 tablespoons)
- Avocado (2 cups of flesh)

Preparation:

This preparation should last about 15 minutes. Prepare simple syrup from water and sugar. Blend avocado flesh with simple syrup, lime rind, lime juice, and a bit of salt until smooth. Pour the mixture into the molds and freeze for about 4+ hours.

<h1 style="text-align:center">Recipe No. 75</h1>

You need:

- 8 ice pop molds
- Egg yolks (3 eggs)
- Cornstarch (¼ cup)
- Coconut milk (3 cups)
- A bit of salt
- Vanilla extract (2 tablespoons)
- Sugar ($2/3$ cup)
- Avocado (1½, peeled and pitted)
- Lime juice (1/ tablespoons)

Preparation:

This preparation should last about 25 minutes. Take a saucepan and mix cornstarch with salt and sugar. Then add coconut milk and stir until sugar and salt dissolve. Then whisk in egg yolks and place the saucepan on the heater. Cook this mixture over a medium heat and whisk it until you see the first bubbles. Decrease the heat and continue to cook and whisk for about one minute. Then remove the saucepan from the heater and stir in vanilla extract. Take a blender and mix avocado puree, lime juice, and this coconut mixture from the saucepan. Blend until smooth and pour the mixture into the molds. Freeze the molds for 6+ hours.

Recipe No. 76

You need:

- 8 ice pop molds
- Cocoa powder ($^{1/3}$ cup)
- Maple syrup (½ cup)
- Avocado (1 large, ripe)
- Vanilla extract (1 tablespoon)
- A bit of salt
- Almond milk (1 ½ cup)

Preparation:

This preparation should last about 15 minutes. Take the avocado flesh out and place it in the blender. Add all the ingredients and blend until smooth. Pour this mixture into the molds and freeze for 8+ hours.

Recipe No. 77

You need:

- 4 ice pop molds
- Greek yogurt (½ cup)
- Almond milk (½ cup)
- Avocado (1 ripe)
- Vanilla extract (1 tablespoon)
- Honey (2 tablespoons)
- Matcha powder
- Water (2 tablespoons)

Preparation:

This preparation should last about 10 minutes. Take the avocado flesh and put it in the blender together with almond milk, Greek yogurt, and water. When blended, add matcha powder, vanilla extract, and honey. Take the molds and pour this mixture into them. Freeze the molds overnight and tomorrow morning your popsicles will be ready.

Recipe No. 78

You need:

- 4 ice pop molds
- 1 Avocado
- 1 banana
- Greek yogurt (½ cup)

Preparation:

This preparation should last about 5 minutes. Take a blender and mix all the ingredients until smooth. Pour the mixture into the molds and freeze the molds for about 8 hours.

VII POPSICLES MADE WITH LEMON JUICE

Recipe No. 79

You need:

- 6 ice pop molds
- Lemon juice (1 tablespoon)
- Mango chunks (1 cup)
- Raspberries (½ cup)
- Cubed seeded watermelon (2 cups)

Preparation:
This preparation should last about 15 minutes. Blend all the ingredients until smooth. Pour the mixture into molds and insert wooden sticks. Freeze the pops for about 4 hours.

Recipe No. 80

You need:

- 12 ice pop molds
- Water (3 cups, cold)
- Frozen lemonade concentrate (1 i.e. 12 ounces)
- Frozen sliced strawberries (1 i.e. 16 ounces)

Preparation:

This preparation should last for about 15 minutes. Stir together water and lemonade concentrate. Put strawberries into the blender and mix until smooth. Mix lemonade and stir it into the lemonade. Take this mixture and pour it into the molds. Place them in the freezer for 4+ hours.

Recipe No. 81

You need:

- 8 ice pop molds
- Lemon juice (1 tablespoon)
- Sugar (¼ cup)
- Fresh raspberries (½ cup)
- Watermelon (2½ cups, cubed, seeded)

Preparation:

This preparation should last about 15 minutes. You should take all the ingredients and put them, one by one, into the blender. Then blend them until the mixture becomes smooth. This smooth mixture then goes into the molds and the sticks should be inserted. Put the molds into the freezer for more than 4 hours.

<h1 style="text-align:center">Recipe No. 82</h1>

You need:

- 6 ice pop molds
- Lemon zest (½ teaspoon)
- Lemonade (1¼ cups)
- Honey (3 tablespoons)
- Blueberries (1½ cups)
- Cider vinegar (2 tablespoons)

Preparation:

This preparation should last about 20 minutes. Take a bowl and put blueberries, vinegar, honey, and lemon zest in it. Cover it with the wrap for the microwave and poke a few holes in it. Place the bowl into the microwave for about 2 minutes. Then stir it and microwave again for 1 minute. Take the mixture out of the microwave and cool it for 10 minutes. Sieve the mixture and then add the lemonade. Fill in the molds with the mixture. After this follows the freezing process which lasts about 6 hours.

Recipe No. 83

You need:

- 12 ice pop molds
- Lemon juice made of 1 lemon
- Vanilla extract (¼ teaspoon)
- Sugar (¼ cup)
- Fresh orange juice (¼ cup)
- Peaches (1¼ pounds, halved and pitted)

Preparation:

This preparation should last about 15 minutes. Chop the peaches into pieces and mix it with lemon juice, orange juice, and sugar. Blend this mixture until it gets smooth and mix it with vanilla. Place the mixture into the molds, freeze the molds a bit and then place the sticks. Then continue the freezing process for 2 hours.

Recipe No. 84

You need:

- 8 ice pop molds
- Water (3 tablespoons)
- Lemon juice (1 tablespoon)
- Sugar (3 tablespoons)
- Cranberry juice (¼ cup)
- Strawberries (2 cups)

Preparation:

This preparation should last about 15 minutes. Take a blender and place these ingredients in it: sugar, lemon juice, strawberries, cranberry juice, and water and blend until smooth. Pour the mixture into the molds and freeze for one hour, then place the sticks and continue the freezing process for about 2 hours.

Recipe No. 85

You need:

- 8 ice pop molds
- Finely slivered fresh mint leaves (1 tablespoon)
- Cantaloupe (1 small)
- Water (½ cup)
- Sugar (¼ cup)
- Lemon juice (¼ cup)

Preparation:

This preparation should last about 20 minutes. Take the cantaloupe and cut it in half. Remove all the seeds and scoop out the flesh. Take a blender and put this cantaloupe into it. Blend until it becomes smooth. You will need here 1¼ cup of the cantaloupe. Take the saucepan with water and sugar. Let it boil a bit and stir in mint. Then remove the saucepan from the heat and let it cool a bit. Mix the cantaloupe with this mint syrup and lemon juice. Now, you only have to pour the final mixture into the molds and let it freeze for about 2 hours.

VIII POPSICLES MADE WITH SPECIAL FLAVORS AND AROMAS

Recipe No. 86

You need:

- 6 ice pop molds
- Fresh basil (2 tablespoons, finely minced)
- Frozen peaches (1 piece / 16 ounces, sliced)
- Peach nectar (2 cups)

Preparation:

This preparation should last about 10 minutes. Blend all the ingredients until smooth and pour the mixture into the molds. Keep them in the freezer for 4+ hours.

Recipe No. 87

You need:

- 8 ice pop molds or plastic cups
- Sugar (1 cup)
- Fruit favored gelatin (1 package / 3 ounces)
- Flavored soft drink mix (1 package, unsweetened)
- Water (2 cups, boiling)
- Water (2 cups, cold)

Preparation:

This preparation should last about 15 minutes. You should dissolve gelatin, sugar, and soft drink mix in boiling water. Then stir it in cold water and pour into the ice pop molds or plastic cups. Put them in the freezer until firm. Insert sticks and return to the freezer to stay there until completely frozen (4+ hours).

Recipe No. 88

You need:

- 6 ice pop molds
- Warm peanut butter (1½ teaspoons)
- Milk (2 cups, cold)
- Instant banana pudding (1 package / 3.5 ounces)

Preparation:

This preparation should last about 10 minutes. Take a bowl and pour the milk into it, then whisk the pudding mix until dissolved. Leave it to rest for about 5 minutes. Take the peanut butter and mash it into the pudding. Pour the mixture into pop molds and while doing this tap the molds on the hard surface to be sure that no air bubbles are left inside. Leave the molds in the freezer for about 5 hours.

Recipe No. 89

You need:

- 16 paper cups
- Cold water (1 cup)
- Boiling water (2 cups)
- Ice cubes
- Sugar (1 cup)
- Lime flavored gelatin (1 package)
- Strawberry flavored gelatin (1 package)
- Semi-sweet chocolate chips (3 tablespoons)
- Cream cheese (4 ounces, softened)
- Whipped topping (1 ½ cups, thawed)

Preparation:

This preparation should last for about 35 minutes. Take a bowl and mix lime gelatin, $^{1/3}$ cup of sugar, and 1 cup of boiling water for about 2 minutes. Then add some ice cubes to ½ cup of cold water to fill ¾ of the cup and mix it with the first mixture and stir until all the ice cubes are completely melted. Place this new mixture into the refrigerator for about 25 minutes. Mix $^{1/3}$ cup of sugar with the cup of boiling water, and strawberry gelatin. Repeat the same process with the ice cubes, pour it into the paper cups and freeze them for about 20 minutes. Put ½ tablespoon of chocolate chips into this gelatin in each cup. The rest of the sugar should be mixed with cream cheese with mixer until smooth. Then add the spread the topping over the gelatin in these cups. Previously prepared lime gelatin should be poured over the cream cheese mixture. Afterward, insert the wooden sticks into each cup and freeze them for about 3 hours.

Recipe No. 90

You need:

  - 12 ice pop molds
  - Water (2 cups)
  - Vanilla extract (¼ teaspoon)
  - Sugar (½ cup)
  - Vanilla cream soda (1 bottle / 20 ounces)

Preparation:

This preparation should last about 10 minutes. Take a bowl and whisk cream soda in it until it no longer has bubbles. On the other side, heat sugar with water in a saucepan and stir it until the sugar is completely dissolved. Mix cream soda with this sweet water and vanilla extract by the mixer. We are almost finished now, just pour this mixture into the molds, insert the sticks and freeze for about 5 hours.

You need:

- 10 ice pop molds

- Sugar (½ cup)

- Salt (¼ teaspoon)

- 4 Mangos (1 peeled, seeded, and diced and 3 peeled, seeded, and cut into chunks)

- Fresh chopped basil (1 tablespoon)

- Limes (2, juiced)

- Cayenne pepper (½ teaspoon)

Preparation:

This preparation should last about 20 minutes. You should blend all the ingredients except sugar and diced mango. When the mixture is smooth, add the sugar and stir it until dissolved. Then fold the diced mango into this mixture and that is all. Then place this mixture into the molds and freeze them for more than 14 hours.

You need:

- 10 ice pop molds
- A bit of salt
- Half-and-half cream (1 cup)
- Hot brewed coffee (2½ cups)
- Vanilla extract (¼ teaspoon)
- Sugar (5 tablespoons)
- Unsweetened cocoa powder (2 tablespoons)

Preparation:

This preparation should last about 10 minutes. You should whisk cocoa, sugar, and coffee until sugar becomes dissolved. Then mix it with half-and-half cream, vanilla, and a bit of salt. Place the mixture into the molds, place the sticks and freeze for about 6 hours.

Recipe No. 93

You need:

- 10 ice pop molds
- Lime juice (2 tablespoons)
- Sugar (2 tablespoons)
- Blueberries (1 cup)
- Watermelon (3¾ cups, chopped, seedless)

Preparation:

This preparation should last about 10 minutes. You should blend lime juice and sugar with the watermelon. Place the blueberries into the molds (equally divided among the molds) and pour this watermelon mixture over the blueberries. Then freeze the molds for about 6+ hours.

Recipe No. 94

You need:

- 8 ice pop molds
- Grated fresh ginger (1 teaspoon)
- Freshly grated lime zest (1 teaspoon)
- Sugar ($2/3$ cup)
- Lime juice ($1/3$ cup)
- Green food color (1 drop)
- Kiwi (2, peeled and sliced)
- Water ($1^{1/3}$ cups)

Preparation:

This preparation should last about 30 minutes. You should take a saucepan and mix water, sugar, lime zest, and ginger in it. Then stir this mixture over the high heat until it boils. Remove it from the heat and cool it a bit. This syrup should be strained through a fine sieve and then add the lime juice and the food color. Take the molds and place the slices of kiwi on the sides of the molds. Then pour this mixture over the kiwis and freeze the molds for about 1 hour. Insert the sticks and return to the freezer for 1 hour more.

Recipe No. 95

You need:

- 10 ice pop molds
- Raspberries (1 cup)
- Blueberries (1 ½ cup)
- Limeade (2 cups)

Preparation:

This preparation should last about 10 minutes. Place some fruits in every mold then pour limeade over the fruits. Put molds in the freezer for about one hour, insert sticks and continue the freezing process for about 6+ hours.

Recipe No. 96

You need:

- 8 ice pop molds
- Superfine sugar (¼ cup)
- Milk ($1/3$ cup)
- Confectioners' sugar (1 tablespoon)
- Heavy cream (¼ cup)
- Strongly brewed coffee (1 ¾ cup)

Preparation:

This preparation should last about 20 minutes. Take a small bowl and pour the coffee, milk, and add the sugar. Whisk until sugar becomes dissolved. Take another bowl and mix the cream and confectioners' sugar. Divide the first mixture among the molds and then add the cream mixture. Freeze the molds for about 5 hours.

Recipe No. 97

You need:

- 10 ice pop molds
- Honey (2 tablespoons)
- Kiwi (6 pieces)
- Pineapple (1 whole)

Preparation:

This preparation should last about 10 minutes. Take pineapple chunks, kiwi, and honey and place them in the blender. Blend them until smooth. Place pieces of kiwis into every mold and pour this mixture over the kiwis. Freeze the molds for about 12+ hour.

Recipe No. 98

You need:

- 6 ice pop molds
- Heavy whipping cream (2 tablespoons)
- Unsweetened yogurt (1 cup)
- Sugar (¼ cup)
- Powdered matcha green tea (4 tablespoons)

Preparation:

This preparation should last about 10 minutes. You should whisk cream and sugar until sugar dissolves. On the other side, mix yogurt with matcha powder. Then mix the two mixtures and pour this new mixture into the molds. Freeze the molds for about 4 hours.

Recipe No. 99

You need:

- 8 ice pop molds
- Honey (3 tablespoons)
- Orange extract (¼ teaspoon)
- Vanilla extract (½ teaspoon)
- Orange juice (1 cup)
- Full fat coconut milk (1 cup)

Preparation:

This preparation should last about 5 minutes. Simply mix all the ingredients in the blender and pour the mixture into the molds. Leave the molds in the freezer and take them out after 6 hours.

Don't miss out!

Visit the website below and you can sign up to receive emails whenever JB Publishing publishes a new book. There's no charge and no obligation.

https://books2read.com/r/B-A-VLZR-OCDWB

BOOKS 2 READ

Connecting independent readers to independent writers.